Mrs. McCartney's Liverpool Limericks

(and other random Irish haikus)

Dr. Angie McCartney

With illustrations by
Digital Diva Ruth McCartney

Scan to visit Angie's Empire of Books,
Tea, Wine, CBD and Podcast!
Updated with new locations & people
June 17th 2024.

LETTER FROM HER MAJESTY QUEEN CAMILLA

BIRKHALL

25th April, 2024

Dear Angie,

So many thanks for your kind letter. I would be delighted to receive a copy of your book, "Angie McCartney's Liverpool Limericks" – how thoughtful of you!

Thank you also for your generous words about my Reading Room. I am very glad that you are enjoying the site...!

With my best wishes

Camilla R

DEDICATION

Thank you to my trusty team of son-in-law Martin Nethercutt and daughter Ruth McCartney at McCartney-Multimedia.com for their illustration, marketing, PR and technical skills in helping me tell the story of The Fab Four and our hometown of Liverpool in anapestic trimeter. (That's posh for Limerick format.)

CONTENTS

THE HISTORY OF LIMERICKS

Limericks are a type of verse which began in England about the 18th century, or maybe even earlier.

They are usually of a humorous nature, often very vulgar and raunchy, and sometimes only fit for those not of a prim and proper disposition.

Generally performed by men, about women, back in the days when the fair sex was not as emancipated as we are now.

Wikipedia shows a lengthy history, dating back centuries, from the days of the Vikings, and if you so wish, you can delve into the back story via our handy dandy QR code.

Or if you would simply like to be entertained, perhaps you will enjoy the following pages.

Popularized by poet Edward Lear in the 19th century, and used primarily by males and pertaining to females, they usually followed a five-line pattern.

The dictionary describes them in high-falutin complex words, but a simplified version is:

DA DADA DA DADA DA **DA**
DA DADA DA DADA DA **DA**
DA DADA DA **DA**
DA DADA DA **DA**
DA DADA DA DADA DA DA

Or simply: AABBA (Remind you of anyone?)

As my readers will know by now, I tend to let my mind wander, (although I sometimes think it shouldn't be allowed out on its own,)

I have put together a few of my choice Limericks to introduce to children, parents and grandparents, a brand-new way of discovering the history of our fair city of Liverpool, and a few of the people connected "in my life," such as the Fab Four and their entourage which I hope will amuse and inform you.

So sit back, laugh, groan, wince, and share if you dare.

So even though they began in England,
here's a digital etching by Ruth of Limerick
Castle in Ireland (just to keep us all
confused)…oh, and a QR Code to scan
with your phone's camera in case you'd like
to learn more.

Dr. Angie

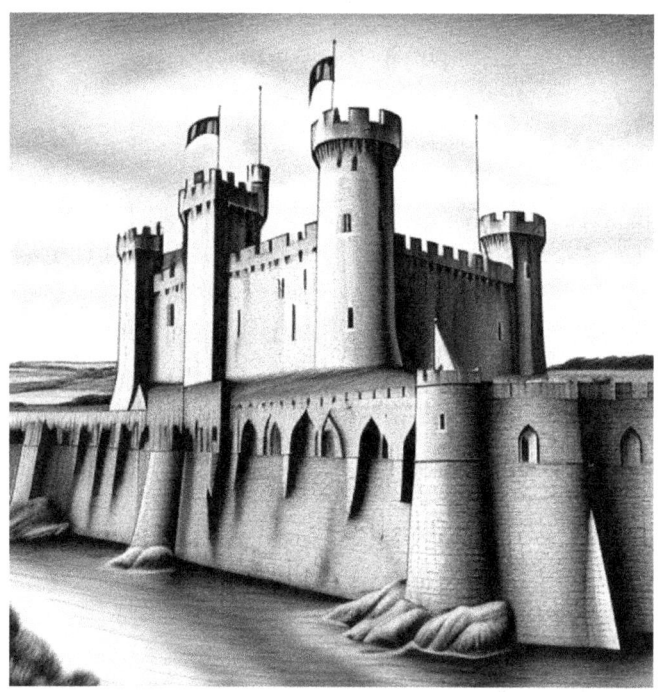

Scan to learn more about
the history of Limericks

CHAPTER 1 - LIVERPOOL HISTORY

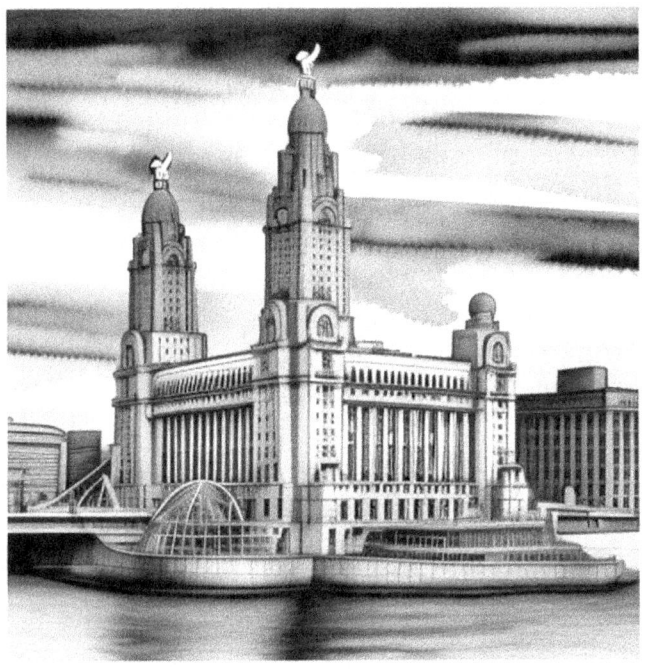

In Liverpool, history runs deep
A city with memories to keep
From its maritime past
To the first Beatles' blast
Our city's still top of the heap

From the Fab Four to football's fierce chase
In Liverpool's spirit, you'll trace
A city so proud
In voices so loud
As The British Invasion's birthplace

At Anfield, the "Reds" take the stage
Scousers' passion, a loud roaring rage
With each thunderous cheer
Their anthem sincere
They'll not walk alone on this stage

Mersey shores, where dreams still unfold
The 'pool's story in red and in gold
From Shankly to Klopp
From the pubs to the Kop
Anfield's heartbeat a tale to be told

Everton, where the Toffees play true
A tale etched in the Mersey's blue hue
From Dixie's grand grace
To Prince Rupert's embrace
Goodison's legacy has come through

By Mersey's edge blue flags still fly
Everton players still reach for the sky.
With passion aflame
In soccer's grand game
Goodison is where dreams never die.

Author's note: In 2024, after 132 years at Goodison Park, Everton are set to leave the stadium and relocate to the Bramley-Moore Dock site, after which the Goodison Park site will be redeveloped.

CHAPTER 2 - THE FAB FOUR

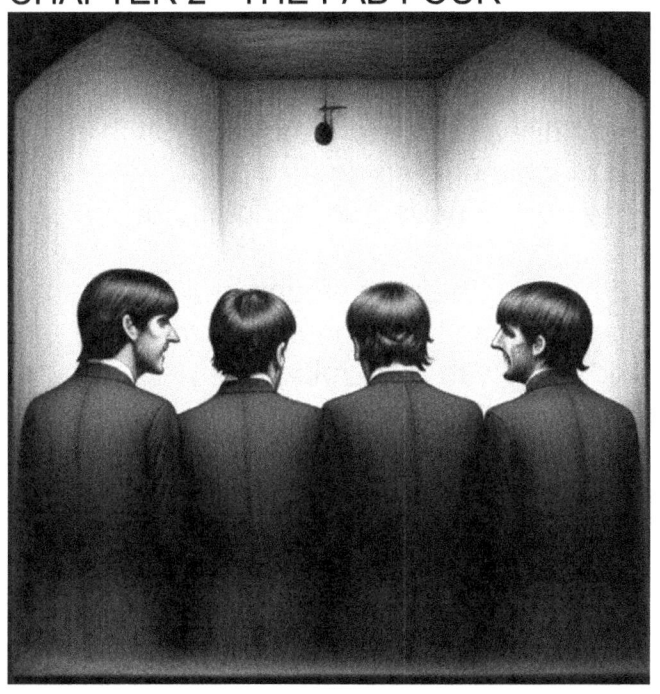

JOHN LENNON

John Winston he started it all
As early fans surely recall
Then along came the others
They bonded like brothers
Through problems they always stood tall

John's wit 'n charm part of his game
He'd have never "imagined" the fame
"War Is Over" and "Peace"
Spread emotional release
And music was never the same

John Lennon, a man of great might
With his words, he'd inspire and ignite
From his youth, he'd create
So much music so great
He would conquer the world and delight

With Yoko, they both found new loves
They bonded like two turtle doves
And each with their voice
Found a way to rejoice
Till his tragic end took him above

PAUL McCARTNEY
Paul's talent still burns ever bright
With his music he reached a new height
"Yesterday," "Let It Be"
Let his talents run free
And that voice, like a warm summer night

In The Beatles, he played a key role
With his bass, and his voice and his soul
He could charm all the gals
And win over male pals
Making fans happy – the goal

His creation, it never will stop
And with Wings he remained at the top
"Maybe I'm Amazed"
Is a song that's still praised

And his talent's the cream of the crop

So Paul has his groupies for sure
And daily they grow more and more
They follow him loyally
And treat him like royalty
With most of them wishing for more

Now with whimsy and joy, kids can ride
With ol' Grandude's compass the guide
A submarine green
Tryin' to keep he world clean
Writing kids' books keeps Paul in his stride

RINGO STARR
Ringo Starr is a drummer so fine
Thru his beats, he dictates perfect time
From the Dingle he came
Helped the Beatles win fame
With his rhythms, forever in line

With his sticks, he would keep up the beat
His style so unique and so neat
His humour and quips
Bring a smile to our lips
And his outlook is always a treat

His voice, too, then made a breakthrough
'Bout a submarine, Yellow in hue
And his All-Starr Band

Still rings out 'cross the land
With a rock 'n' roll legendary crew

So let's give busy Ringo a shout
He rocks and he rolls without doubt
Like Paul he's a lefty
As a drummer that's hefty
So he never has time to chill out

GEORGE HARRISON
From "Something" to "Here Comes the
Sun"
The hearts of the public he won
He shone on guitar
Then moved on to sitar
A genius second to none

Spirituality part of his soul
 "My Sweet Lord," truly showed us his goal
With The Wilburys he'd play
Have some fun on the way
To make people smile was his role

So friends we were lucky to hear
Dear George, a musician so dear
His heart-warming smile
Raised us up for a while
Remembering him each time we hear

CHAPTER 3 - EARLY DAYS

Jacaranda's brick walls may be gone
But the mem'ries forever live on
The Beatles took flight
On a hot August night
And today they're still second to none

Then Hamburg was where it all started
From The Jac once the boys had departed
They honed all their skills
And strengthened their wills
And from then on they never were parted

In Hamburg around Beatles-Platz
There followed some management chats
The locals admired them
Immediately hired them
To play as their in-house cool cats

They went back downstairs in the Cavern
A dark, dingy smokey old tavern
What Brian uncovered
We all soon discovered
That nothing but fun were they havin'

The Cavern was part of the plan
Where Merseyside's music began
Once they came on the stage
Rocked the crowd with their rage

Their music just thrilled every fan

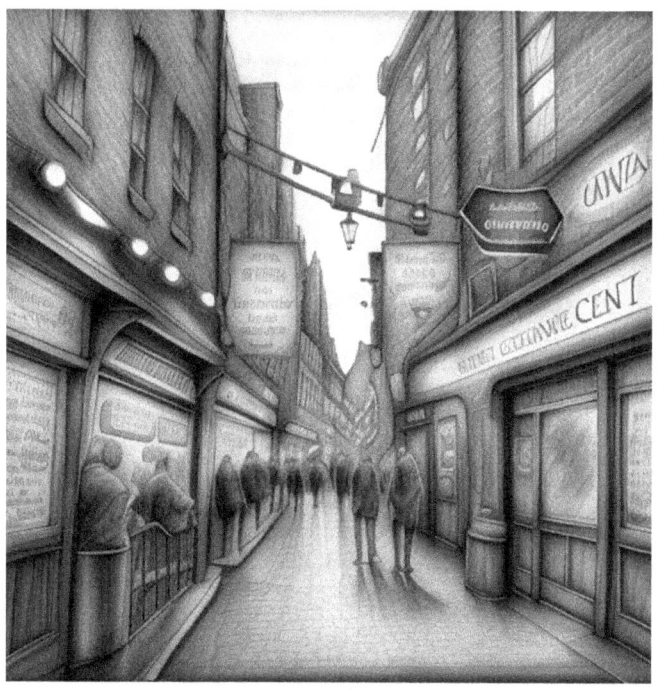

The Cavern was stuffy and hot
But the fans really loved it a lot
A shrine from the start
Music came from the heart
And its image was part of the plot

In Woolton was held a Church fair
With talents exceedingly rare
With St. Peter's the venue
Began the lads' menu

Beginning new sounds in the air

John Lennon first hooked up with Paul
His interest was seemingly small
'Til Paul's "Johnny B Goode"
Made John feel that they could
Go forward and surely enthrall

In time their togetherness grew
And gradually both of them knew
Together they'd find
They were two of a kind
Like brothers they were, through and
through

With George and then Ringo they sprouted
And in no time at all people shouted
Their fame it was spreading
To the top they were heading
Their future was bright and undoubted

Brian Epstein, with vision and grace
Polished the band's public face
Though they hesitated
Their success escalated
Their image now firmly in place

Paul then took over the bass
His leadership firmly in place
The four of them fitted

In tune and quick witted
With Merseyside bands in a race

From "Yesterday" on thru "Let It Be"
Paul's melodies set spirits free
With "Hey Jude" in tow
He made hearts all aglow
A musical master is he

Ringo joined them and he was so bright
With rhythm, he'd dance through the night
With Beatles, he'd play
In their fabulous way
A star in the rock-and-roll light

His beats kept the music in line
A talent so rare and divine
In the band's joyful tale
His smile would prevail
With charm and a wit so benign

Those haircuts sure started a craze
Which some thought was only a phase
But they spread far and wide
Folks would wear them with pride
They just never ceased to amaze

The 'suits' didn't favour their act
They just told them "no" without tact
But George Martin demurred

And made sure they were heard
Yes, and still Decca lost THAT contract

With strings, horns, effects & much more
Sir George's light touch would ensure
New boundaries, ideas
They became pioneers
And many new styles they'd explore

The Beatles became quite the fashion
And clothes were their newly found passion
In their slick Chelsea boots
And their collarless suits
And Ringo with fingers a-flashin'

The Royal Variety they wowed
All their parents were ever so proud
They acted like fools
John said "rattle yer jewels"
And the after-show got pretty loud

Their "road" food was plain at the least
On baked beans or butties they'd feast
But as they matured
And became more assured
Their intake of veggies increased

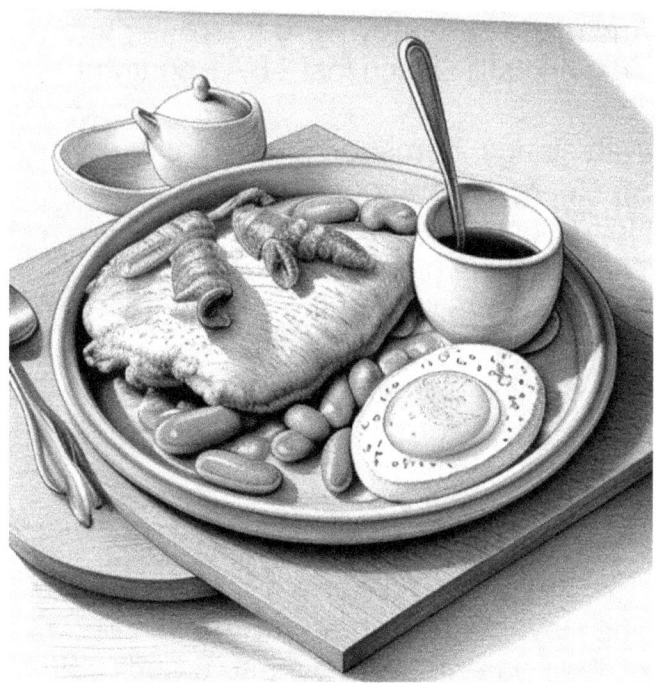

Would now be a good time to suggest a nice cuppa Mrs.McCartney's Tea? We have 14 fab flavours and some other fun books at the link below (scan with your phone camera.)

CHAPTER 4 - BEATLES IN AMERICA

2/9/64

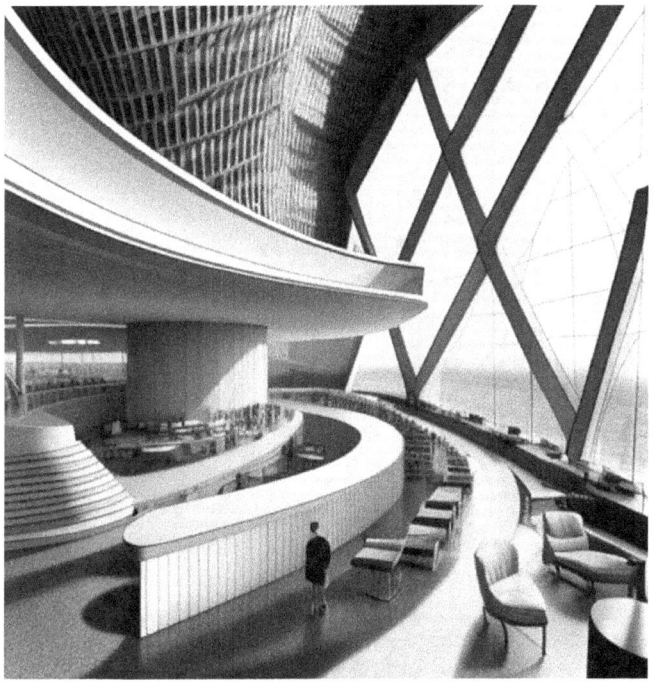

The screaming fans stormed JFK
And made it a memorable day
But how could they know
That Ed Sullivan's show
Would open up ALL USA?

2/9/64
THE ED SULLIVAN THEATER
The Ed Sullivan Theater, renowned
In New York a true hallowed ground
Where legends have played
On its stage, dreams displayed
With a history that truly astounds

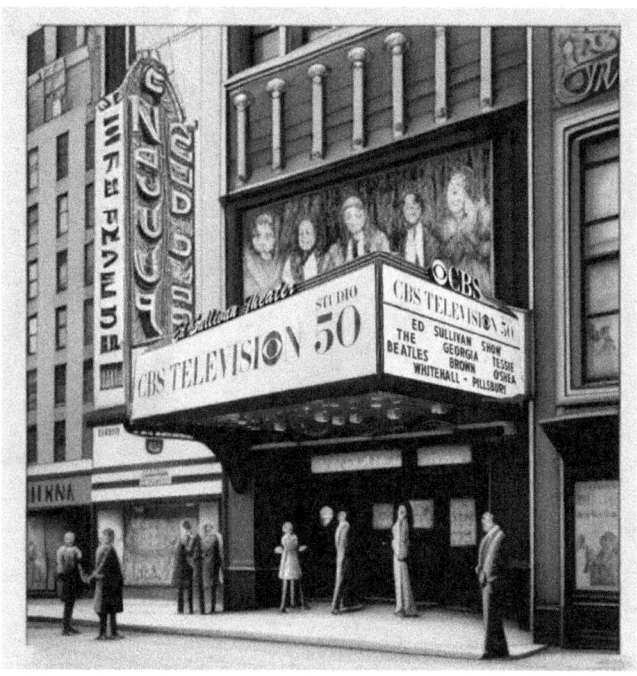

In the heart of the city so bright
Ed Sullivan Theater's a sight
Where laughter and song
Have danced all night long

In the Big Apple's e're glowing limelight

2/12/64
Performing at Carnegie Hall
Was a place where the boys had a ball
Their welcome was vocal
From the audience local
'Twas a fabulous evening for all

8/25/64

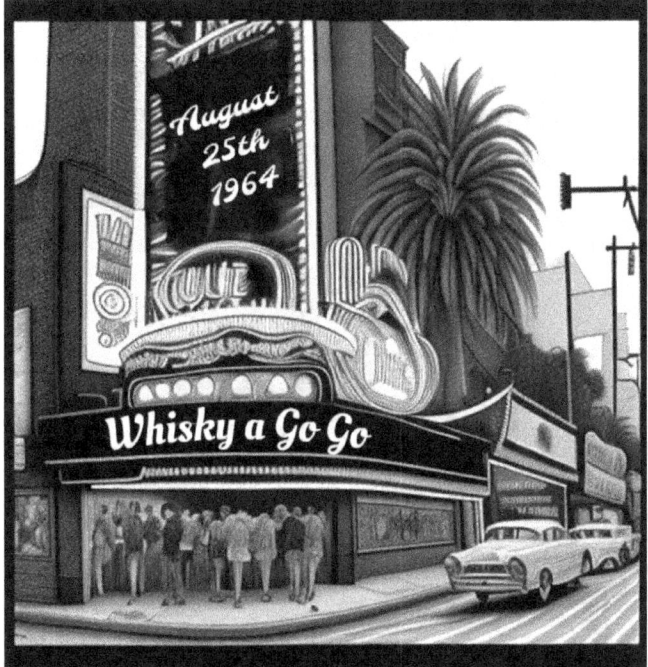

Jayne Mansfield they met at The Whisky
Which made them all feel a bit frisky

They needed security
To maintain their purity
To behave otherwise was too risky

8/15/65

At Shea Stadium a frenzy took flight
Fans' fervor, a magical sight
In the warm summer air
Those melodies rare
The Fabs' legend it soared to new heights

8/29+30/65

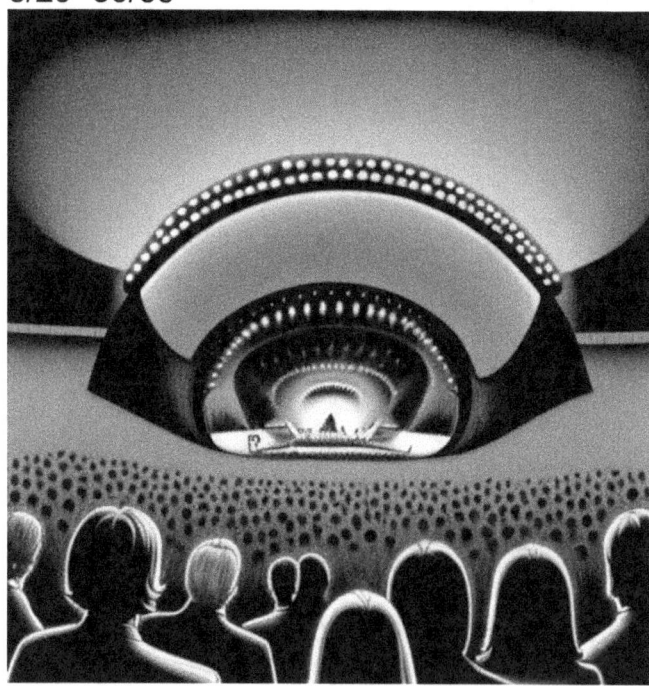

In Hollywood Bowl's August breeze
Bob Eubanks, the maestro would please
Tens of thousands of girls
Who were clutching their pearls
As The Beatles brought them to their knees

8/28/66

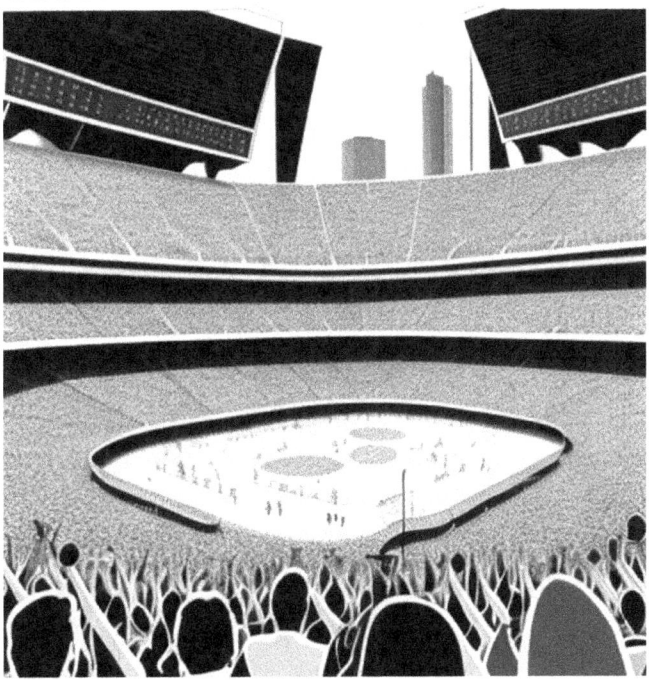

They played at L.A.'s Dodger Stadium
A thrill, like the London Palladium
Armoured van cops took care

That they got out of there
A dangerous gig, just like radium

8/29/66
At Candlestick park where it ended
The screams were so shrill they offended
The boys then agreed
That indoors was their need
Then with studio work they transcended

CAPITOL RECORDS

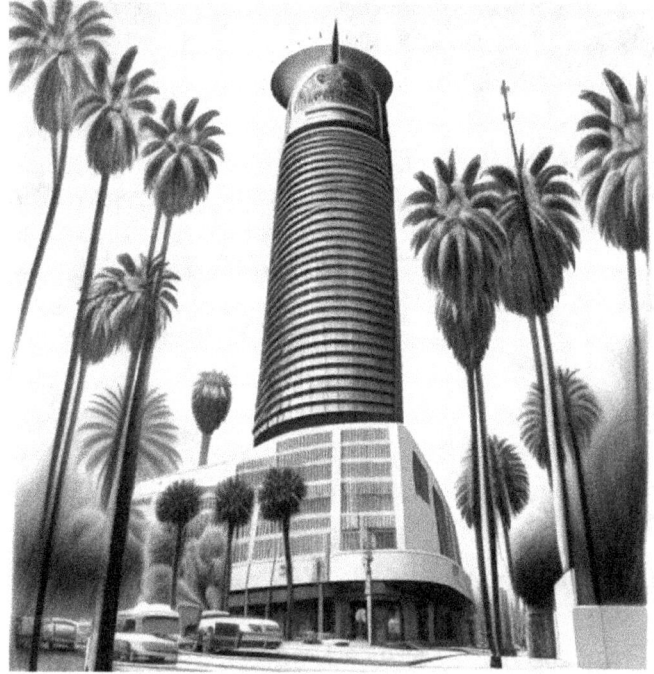

The Capitol Tower in L.A.
A monument still to this day

A tourist's delight
People gaze at the sight
With the walk of fame stars on display

CHAPTER 5 - SOME OF THE BEATLE PEOPLE

ASTRID KIRCHHER
Astrid, in Hamburg, had flair
With scissors that cut through the air
The Fabs style, from their friend
Really started a trend
Defined a new look, oh so rare

In art and in fashion, she led
Creating a style that widespread
With a touch of her grace
In Hamburg's embrace
She styled many trendy young heads

BARBARA BACH
Barbara Bach, so stunning and bright
Found love with Ringo, a star of the night
In the world of the beat
Their love was complete
A bond that felt perfectly right

Through the years, their love has held
strong
In a life filled with music and song
With Ringo by her side
It has been a wild ride
In Beatles' legacy they both belong

She and Ringo a union so sweet
A love story that can't be beat
In life's symphony
Remains love's harmony
Together, their lives are replete

BILLY J. KRAMER
Billy J. - a huge Liverpool star,
With the Beatles, he toured near and far.
He and Epstein were keen,
And topped charts - such a dream,
His voice and his looks, raised the bar

BILLY PRESTON
Billy Preston a man of great skill
With his music he'd give us a thrill
He'd smile and he'd sing
Oh the joy he would bring
And the Fabs thought their boy was 'dead
brill'

He performed on piano so fine
With "Nothing From Nothing" divine
With the Stones too he'd play
Having fun night and day
Sometimes needing to keep them in line

Smiling Billy was always on hand
To fill in on keyboards when planned

With his bright winning smile
He'd be there for a while
Ever ready when called on demand

With The Beatles he'd happily stand
His talents were much in demand
And on "Don't Let Me Down"
He sure went to town
Those keyboards were at his command

BRIAN EPSTEIN
When Brian first witnessed the boys
In a cellar so choc full of noise
It kindled a spark
Like a beam in the dark
Which would bring us all so many joys

This charming young man known as
"Eppy"
Had a spring in his step that was peppy
But back in the day
'Twasn't cool to be gay
Although he was smart and so preppy

Lunchtime sessions they played at The
Cavern
A dark, dingy smoky old tavern
But Brian uncovered
What we all soon discovered
That nothing but fun they were havin'

He started to take them in hand
And cleaned up the look of the band
They fought it a bit
Then they gave it a hit
And in no time their image was grand

If he could be with us today
And see how it's come into play
As folks are more tender
Displaying their gender
And they know it's OK to be gay

CYNTHIA LENNON
Cyn Lennon a lady so fair
Her devotion was lasting and rare
As a mother and wife
She was subject to strife
But a lifetime's devotion she'd share

Her art she'd create and design
Such talent forever a sign
Then her books told the story
Of the loss of the glory
When her life was no longer divine

In the twilight of life, she found peace
The Mother-Son bond never ceased
With Julian there

To fulfill her prayer
A love of 2 hearts, such release

Through all the tough chapters, they
shared
As previous feuds were repaired
The memories so tender
Love's enduring splendor
This Mother & Child were so rare

FREDA KELLY
Freda Kelly, a gal who's all heart
In the early days playing her part
Their Fan Club she ran
With the strength of a man
It was never too early to start

So now let us all give a cheer
For Freda, a fan so sincere
Her great dedication
Earned her great admiration
And her stories remain ever dear

The mem'ries she kept oh so clear
She was faithful throughout their career
Ryan White's "Good Ol' Freda"
Delighted the reader
*And I'm proud to have had a cameo part in
it so I don't give a toss whether the last line
rhymes or not.*

GEOFF EMERICK

Geoff Emerick, a talent profound
Aural magic he brought to their sound
With Geoff's brilliant touch
Their records would clutch
A legacy that would astound

In Abbey Road Geoff would preside
Engineering their music with pride
With the Beatles he'd soar
Their sounds he'd explore
And in no time he worked as their guide

From "Revolver" to "Pepper's" delight
Innovations he'd blend, day and night
With EMI's best
The Fab Four impressed
And their musical prowess took flight

Geoff's ears were his main saving grace
Music took him all over the place
His talent was mixing
Many songs he was fixing
To the top of the charts they would race

He helped the boys make their decisions
And often suggested revisions
To line ups and cues
Whether pop, jazz or blues

And lead them to pop's top positions

JAMES MCCARTNEY JR.

Young James is the clan's only lad
And maybe that can't be too bad
His musical flair
Is a talent not rare
When you know who he has for a Dad.

JANE ASHER

British actress Jane Asher so fair
With Paul there was love in the air
But not meant to be
And although sad to see
They ended this great love affair

With her talent on stage and on screen
In the '60s, a prominent queen
Paul's muse and his heart
But they drifted apart
The memory remains evergreen

JIM McCARTNEY

Jimmy Mac, one of life's greatest Dads
Worked so hard to take care of his lads
He cooked and provided
Until they'd decided
To excel in their personal fads

A man of some musical skill
Whose duty was just to fulfill
Met his boys' every need
Until he was freed
Their successes gave Jim such a thrill

JULIA BAIRD
Julia Baird, John's half-sister so dear
In his life, she would bring love and cheer
She shared childhood tales
And their family's travails
But their bond was so truly sincere

Though John's image then became wide
Julia loyally stayed by his side
Through the highs and the strife
In John's tumultuous life
She'd be a constant, and that we can't
hide

LINDA MCCARTNEY
Her spirit so pure and so free
Her lens captured life's vivid glee
Through a photog's trained eye
Under vast, endless skies
Her artistry bloomed like the trees

With Paul by her side, hand in hand,
They formed a harmonious band
To promote veggie fare,

Their message then was so rare,
Linda's goal a compassionate stand.

Now Lovely Linda is watching above
She brought the Mac family such love
Her memory lives on
Even though she is gone
She signifies peace like a dove

Her legacy thrives in our hearts
Linda's passion, a light to impart
Through photography's grace
Her spirit finds place
Memories cherished, she'll never depart

MARTIN NETHERCUTT (my lovely son-in-law)
In the music world Martin's a guide
With Geist Musik, smart thinking can't hide
A composer with flair
In the digital air
Martin's music takes us for a ride

So here's to the maestro at hand
Geist Musik displaying his brand
In each note and each chord
His passion is stored
Creating this magic so grand

With a voice that can soothe and inspire

His songs can ignite such a fire
With passion and flair
His voice fills the air
An artist for all to admire

MARY HOPKIN
Mary Hopkin, a voice oh so charming
With shyness she was quite disarming
Paul produced her first hit
Top of charts she would sit
Quite gentle and never alarming

Her songs would enchant and delight
In the '60s, her talent took flight
With melodies sweet
In each note she would greet
Mary Hopkin's star such a bright light

Though years have passed by since her
prime
Mary's music has stood tests of time
From Apple's embrace
To her own special place
Her legacy's beauty, sublime

MARY McCARTNEY
Mary Macca has talents galore
From food to photography and more
Not just meat free Mondays
She has so many fun days
Her future will surely endure

MAUREEN STARKEY-TIGRETT
Maureen Starkey was Ringo's first wife
Who shared in the boys' crazy life
With love and devotion
Despite the commotion
She navigated the show business strife

The light on her man understood
She coped with it all rather good
A mother of three
Just contented to be
Mo Starkey, a gal from the 'hood

MAY PANG
There once was a beauty, May Pang
Who made Lennon's heart go whiz-bang

Their love didn't last
But that's all in the past
And dear May is still part of our gang

May Pang once became Lennon's Muse
The lady John Winston would choose
With him by her side
Thru' this phase she would guide
'Til an older plan came back to intrude

Their romance was short but so sweet
Time together, a blissful retreat
Their backgrounds contrasting
May's impact long lasting
Her story is one to repeat

May Pang, an artist with flair
Lost Weekend is so debonair
With John Lennon she'd roam
In New York, their new home
A chapter that these two would share

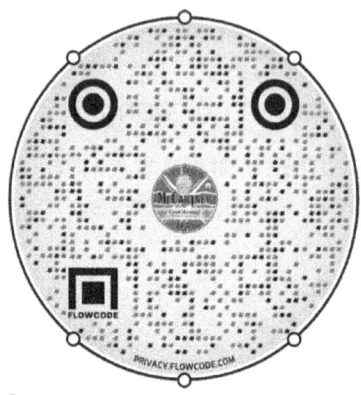

Scan to watch Angie & Ruth interview May Pang on Teaflix Tuesdays

MAHARISHI MAHESH YOGI
Maharishi the Yogi so sage
Taught meditation within the New Age
With transcendental grace
In a calm peaceful space
Shared love from his spiritual stage

In India's land did reside
And through meditation he'd guide
With mantras to chant
From beyond The Levant
His teachings spread far and worldwide

MIKE MCGEAR
Dear Mike even once changed his name
To be separate from big brother's fame

Though he tried more or less
To bamboozle the press
But they labelled him "Mac" just the same

And even though "Lily the Pink"
Was a winner, the folks would still think
Mike was you-know-who's brother
From the same Dad and Mother
But with "Scaffold" he made his own link

NANCY LEE ANDREWS
Nancy Lee Andrews, a model so fair
Engaged once to Ringo, a pair!
In the world of the lens
Their love did commence
A tale of two souls with love shared

Her photography talents did shine
Capturing moments, both yours and mine
And in Ringo's embrace
With a smile on her face
'Twas a story that really seemed fine

Though their paths did eventually part
After having had changes of heart
Nancy Lee's still a muse
Ringo's drummin' on blues
2 successfully parted sweethearts

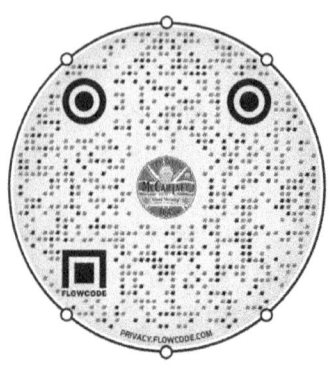

Scan to watch Angie & Ruth interview
Nancy Lee Andrews on Teaflix Tuesdays

NANCY SHEVELL
Now Nancy is Paul's loving wife
She protects him from life's daily strife
Nancy stands beside Paul
And supports over all
And brings so much joy to his life

NEIL ASPINALL
Neil Aspinall, a Beatles mainstay,
Managed their business, day by day.
With loyalty true,
He knew what to do,
Helped the Fab Four's music to stay.

From driving their van in their youth,
To guiding careers, that's the truth.
He wore many hats,

Was a great diplomat,
In their journey, he played a key sleuth.

OLIVIA HARRISON
Olivia a lady so bright
George's love, and his true guiding light
With devotion and grace
In life's endless race
She stood by his side day and night

In Beatles' lore, she found her place
A love story time can't erase
Through music and art
Inside George's heart
Olivia's love filled with grace

With a heart that was tender and warm
In his last days he knew she'd perform
George knew her to be
His sweet harmony
His umbrella in that final storm

PATTI BOYD
Patti Boyd once a model so chic
With elegance, grace and mystique
She caused a sensation
Met George on location
And thus made their coupling unique

With George by her side, they did wed

In a journey where love truly spread
Through the songs he'd compose
Their romance was so close
But to other paths later it led.

Though their ways would eventually split
Their love at the start was a hit
As a muse and a bride
She was at George's side
For a time they were such a good fit.

Though love's journey it had its demand
Patti Boyd, with grace, took a stand
In the '60s she reigned
A beauty unfeigned
A legend in music's own land

PETER ASHER
Peter Asher, a talent so real
His musical bent he'd reveal
From Peter and Gordon
He got so much more done
His productions had worldwide appeal

With a voice that would charm and
astound,
In the '60s, they'd gather around
With "World Without Love"
They rose high above
A melody treasured all round

A producer whose skills were renowned
Worked with stars whose fame had
unwound
Peter Asher's the name
And music's his game
His impact on sound is unbound

RAVI SHANKAR
Through ragas and rhythms conveyed
His culture's harmonious display
Shankar's legacy's vast
And his music will last
Sitar magic cannot be decayed

ROAG BEST
In the 'Pool, there's a fella named Roag,
Who's museum is always in vogue
With collections so vast,
From the Fab Five's great past
If you can decipher Scouse Brogue
At the Casbah, where Beatles began
Mona's son is the man with a plan
With passion and flair,
They'll pamper you there,
And welcome you into their clan!

RUTH MCCARTNEY
Ruth McCartney's a diva so bright
As, she takes on her digital flight,

Dubbed "The Digital Diva"
You may take her or leave her
But she does know her bits from her bytes

The McCartney name, one that's
renowned
In business worlds she's always found
That both vision and drive
In the tech world can thrive
And her internet talents abound

She's a digital mover esteemed
In the world of technology deemed
One with knowledge and grace
In the digital space
In the many Zooms she has convened

SHANNON
In the realm of art, Shannon's the guide
With Beatles' hues canvases glide

On artistshannon.com
Her creations - da bomb
Her paintings, a Fab Four fans' prize

She captures each intimate detail
Buy online & direct - (not at retail)
Through vibrant display
Beatles' spirits at play
Her talents are on a large scale!

SIR GEORGE MARTIN
Sir George was a wizard with sound
Abbey Road - where dreams still abound
A producer so fine
Melodies intertwined
A maestro in his sonic playground

Montserrat an island so grand
Became his creative new land
New music so fine
In the balmy sunshine
Where fresh sonic journeys were planned

STELLA McCARTNEY
In fashion world Stella's the queen
With a flair for style that's serene
Her designs are so chic
Eco-friendly, unique
Her sustainable vision is seen

From a musical lineage, she came
With talent and passion aflame
Her creations delight
Through the day and the night
In Stella's art, there is no shame

With cruelty-free fashion, she's led
A path on which others now tread
Her brain's a sensation
Ethical dedication
Stella's passions so brilliantly spread

STUART SUTCLIFFE
In Hamburg, young Stu took his chance
With Beatles, he joined in a dance
They were knocked off their feet
By a talent so sweet
But art claimed his heart's true expanse

TONY BARROW
Tony Barrow's PR spread the word
With Bill Harry he printed and shared
Even impressing Brian
They sure won by tryin'
Making sure that the youngsters all heard

Tony Barrow, the Beatles' PR man
Would all of their strategy plan
With words, he'd ignite

Starting fame and delight
Raising interest from o'er the land

At the dawn of the young Fab Four's days
Tony's prowess would really amaze
In promoting their charm
He would raise the alarm
A pivotal part of their craze

With charm and with wit, he'd converse
As the boys would compose and rehearse
In the media's embrace,
The lads found their place,
Thanks to Tony's huge talents diverse

VIVEK TIWARY BEATLES AUTHOUR
Vivek, with a passion so bright
Wrote of Epstein, the man in the light
From the Beatles' first songs
To Broadway's grand throngs
His stories bring hits to new heights

YOKO ONO
Yoko Ono, an artist of might,
And with avant-garde vision ignites
A journey profound
In art she'd astound
Pushing boundaries both day and by night

With John Lennon, a story profound
Together, created sweet sounds
In their passion and strife
They'd change art and change life
Yoko Ono's influence, renowned

In the art world, she'd blaze her own trail
Her work, like a ship's mystic sail
A creative life force,
on her chosen course,
Yoko's spirit has never grown frail

CHAPTER 6 - SONGS & CHARACTERS

BILLY SHEARS
And then there was Billy who'd chime
Stepping in as a leader in time
In the "Sgt. Pepper" show
With his voice in the flow
On a musical journey sublime

DEAR PRUDENCE
"Dear Prudence," a song so sincere
Mia Farrow's young sister, oh dear
In the ashram they stayed
In the serenades they played
A tale of retreat, crystal clear

With nature and spirits so free
Prudence needed a way to decree
To come out of her shell
And escape her own spell
The Beatles' plea brought her to be

So "Dear Prudence," please come out to
play
We are waiting for you don't delay
On the White Album's grace
Your name found its place
Awakening the song to this day

ELEANOR RIGBY

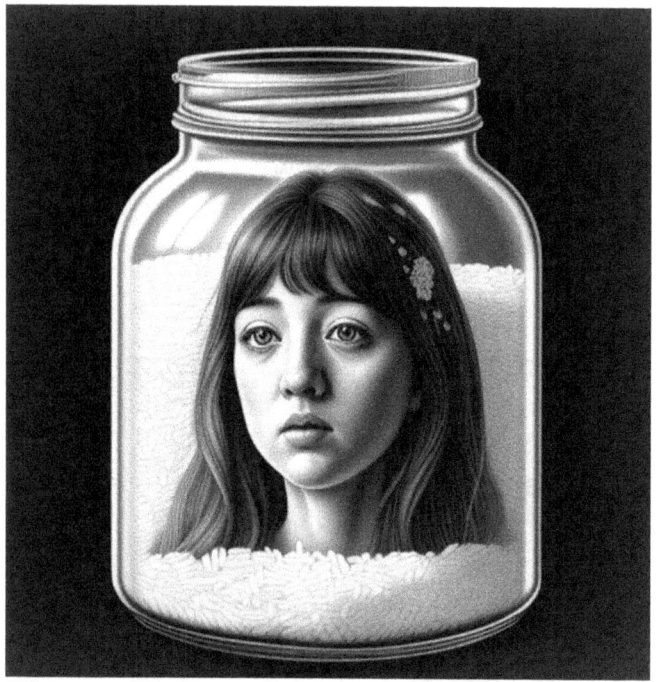

Eleanor Rigby, a figure so stark
So lonely and quiet in the park
Picking up rice
In a world cold as ice
A character both haunting and dark

In her solitude, she'd softly weep
No one to share secrets she'd keep
With her "face" in a jar
And life below par
Eleanor's sorrow ran deep

Now in song her mystery's unsealed
A classic, forever concealed
And now Eleanor's name
Lives in the hall of fame
A portrait of lonely revealed

FOOL ON THE HILL

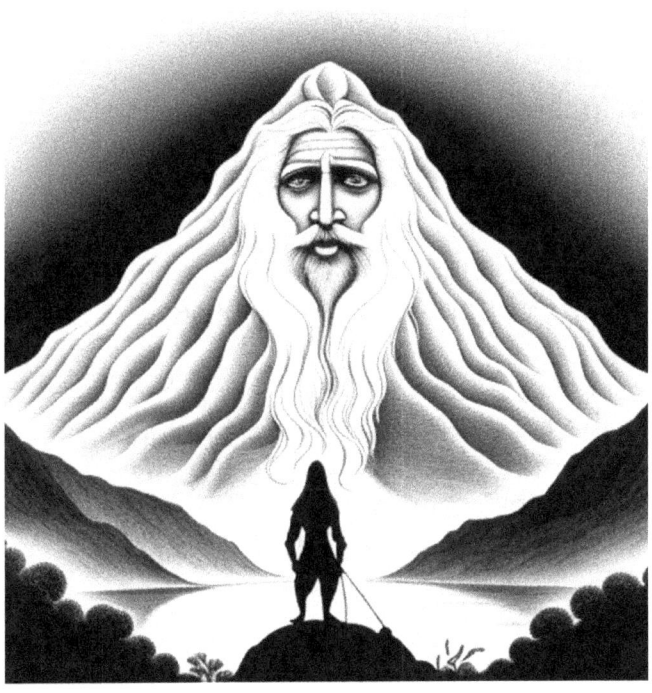

"The Fool on the Hill" so serene
Maharishi, the inspiring scene
Above Rishikesh
He brought ideas afresh
The most peaceful place they'd ever seen

With his wisdom they'd meditate
In the ashram, they'd would contemplate
On the path to the soul
Seeking purpose and goal
And a wonderful stillness create

In India's embrace, they found peace
With his teachings their worries would
cease
Singing "Fool on the Hill"
And their spirits to fill
A song of tranquility and release

LOVELY RITA
In the Beatles' song, Rita WAS spry
As a meter maid catching each guy
With a smile and a wink
She'd make your heart sink
Handing tickets out under the sky

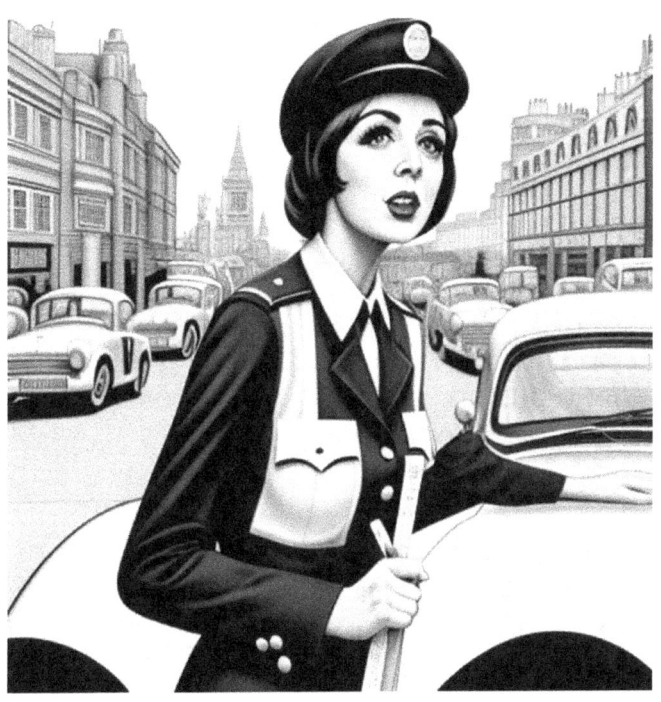

LUCY IN THE SKY WITH DIAMONDS
In a realm where kaleidoscopes fly
"Lucy's sky full with Diamonds" takes high
A lyrical flight
In colors so bright,
A journey that one can't deny

Inspired by young Julian's art
John's creation, a whimsical start
Through surreal terrain
Imagination's domain
Lucy's journey, a mystical part

With melodies floating on high
Lucy travels through realms which defy
Trains leaving stations
For unknown vacations
It's time for some marshmallow pie

MAGICAL MYSTERY TOUR
"Magical Mystery Tour," what a ride
A Beatles' creation, worldwide
With a bus so surreal
In a technicolor deal
To fans on a whimsical stride

From London they went on their way
With music and antics in play
In a psychedelic trance
They'd sing and they'd dance
On this tour that would brighten their day

With surrealism and dreams in the air
"Magical Mystery Tour" was a dare
In the Beatles' grand spree
'Twas a bus trip to see
A giant odyssey ever so rare

MAXWELL'S SILVER HAMMER
Maxwell's Hammer swung with such might
In a tale of dark manner to fright
With a thud and a clang
It would go with a bang

Maxwell's deeds then played out in the night

MR. KITE
Though Pepper had led with such flair
With uniform, mustache and dare
Mr. Kite played his part
With a rhythmical heart
In the minds of the fans they were paired

OCTOPUS'S GARDEN

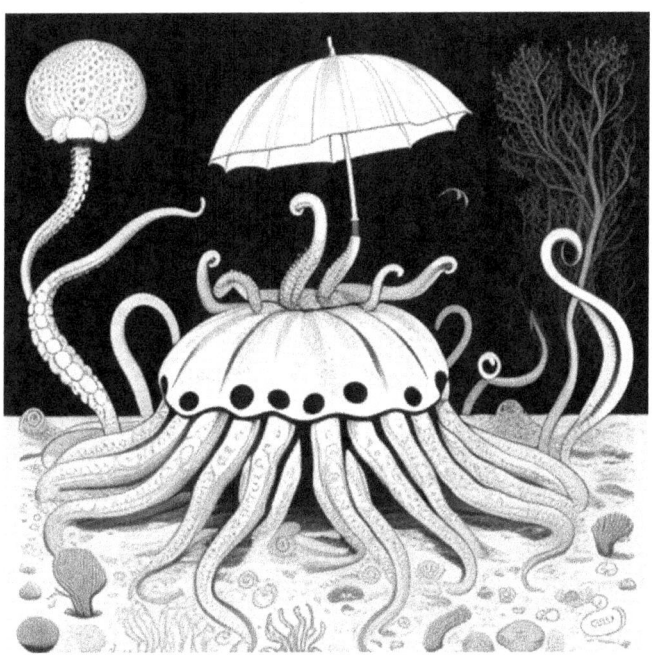

"Octopus's Garden," a song quite sublime
In Beatles' melodies, standing through time
With Ringo its guide
In an undersea ride
A whimsical oceanic rhyme

'Neath the sea, in a coral display,
These long-legged creatures would play
With colorful sights
And aquatic delights
In their garden, they'd frolic and sway

So come join the fun in this scene
With an octopus band, so serene
In the deep blue expanse
You dance and you prance
In "Octopus's Garden" so keen

ROCKY RACCOON
In the town of White Springs he arose
A ballad spun where the folk music flows
With a heart full of ire
He sought his desire
Within "Rocky Raccoon" the tale grows

A triangle in love's strange embrace
Lil Magill and Dan's hearts to erase
With a duel on hand
In that wild frontier land
Rocky's quest a hypotenuse case

So Rocky sought vengeance that day
In the saloon, where guitars would play
And as Gideon's grace
In that Western place
Threw a twist on this frontier display

SEXY SADIE
Sexy Sadie oh boy what a name
In the hall of the White Album's fame
With a twist in her smile
She'd beguile for a while
A mysterious gal in the game

SGT PEPPER
Sergeant Pepper, his crew Kite and Shears
All characters known for their cheers
In the Beatles' grand tale
As music set sail
Brought magic and laughter for years

YELLOW SUBMARINE
A submarine painted bright yellow
Inspiring and fun and so mellow
They made it a movie
Which turned out so groovy
And Ringo became quite the fellow

CHAPTER 7- WINGS

WINGS
The Beatles said "time for a change"
Their fans found this all very strange
Then Paul started Wings
So the world again sings
And Paul then began a new range

So with Linda, Paul then did aspire
To re-light his musical fire
With Denny. and friends
They started new trends
Wings brought us the "Mull of Kintyre."

DENNY LAINE
With Wings Denny Laine was the guy
Who'd improvise, give it a try
He'd give it his all
He was having a ball
And he kept all his chums on a high

He was just such a whiz on guitar
We knew he would go really far
Then he joined up with Wings
On to so many things
And became then a really big star

From "Go Now" to "Mull of Kintyre"
His career just rose higher and higher
From Scotland they rose

And as everyone knows
Wings sure set the fan base on fire

DENNY SEIWELL
Denny Seiwell then joined up with Wings
Giving thrust to their musical flings
Putting jazz riffs on hold
Became part of the fold
And proving what talent he brings

He was known as a drummer with power
Was always the man of the hour
His masterful beat
Got the kids on their feet
His style was the top of the tower

HENRY McCULLOUGH
The adding of Henry's guitar
Showed the guys he was really a star
His interests were critical
And he made them Political
By sending that message afar

JIMMY McCULLOCH
Jimmy's time with the band came and went
But some quality time they all spent
His life short but tragic
He missed so much magic
Cos he made every show an event

JOE ENGLISH

Joe English the drummer took flight
With Wings he gave all of his might
In time he moved on
By the time he was done
He had added some sheer dynamite

LAURENCE JUBER

Oh the joy that this music man brings
He writes and he plays and he sings
He's "Straight Outta Blighty"
His talents are mighty
Read his book called "A Guitar With Wings"

STEVE HOLLEY

Steve Holley joined Wings for a while
Behind them he always would smile
He added some fun
To this Band On The Run
Supporting them all in great style

CHAPTER 8 - BEATLE PLACES

DOVEDALE PRIMARY
Dovedale School was the early location
Where two lads would begin education
George and John's starting ground
The historians found
Where the youngsters began preparation

LIPA aka "THE INNY"
The Liverpool Inny (or "LIPA")
Today is so radically hipper
Most famous students of all
Were both George and Sir Paul
Now it's seen by the everyday tripper

20 FORTHLIN ROAD
In the City, at Forthlin Road's gate
Lived McCartney, a musical great
In his childhood abode
Melodies freely flowed
And the Beatles would soon change his fate

With a guitar a young Paul would be strumming
In his room, where the music kept coming
And with Lennon create
Tunes that would captivate
The whole world once their stardom was

humming

Forthlin Road was where Mike, Paul and
Dad
Lived calmly in this sparse homely pad
With success came the change
Life exciting, but strange
Soon it seemed that the world had gone
mad

Now Forthlin Road stands as a shrine
Where the magic of music did shine
Filled with memories held dear
Childhood homestead so dear
In Scouseland where legends aligned

MENDIPS
In its rooms, where the melodies spun
John's childhood fantasies went on the run
In each corner, a tale
From a Liverpool trail
"Mendips" stands, where Lennon begun

The red-bricked haven, a modest embrace
Witness to Lennon's creative grace
Under Aunt Mimi's care
In the Lancashire air
Was where pop music got to first base

ST. PETER'S CHURCH, WOOLTON

St. Peter's, the Woolton location
Was primed for the Beatles sensation
John Winston met Paul
That's what started it all
And soon they were charming the nation

THE CASBAH CLUB
With Mona Best's Casbah still going
Son Roag is still keeping it flowing
He's fixed it up fine
Now the Fans wait in line
And this popular spot is still growing

HAMBURG
Yes, Hamburg was where it all started
From The Cavern once they'd departed
They honed all their skills
And strengthened their wills
And from then on they never were parted

KAISERKELLAR
Hamburg's Kaiserkeller so grand
The Beatles began making their stand
With music so wild
They rocked like a child
In Germany's rock 'n' roll land
John, Paul, George, Stu. & Peter, they played
In that dank place their skills were displayed

From the Mersey they came
To try claim their fame
And often they barely got paid

Kaiserkeller's vibrant embrace
They honed their craft and found their
space
Their fame soon took flight
In the dim, smoky light
And their legend began to embrace

HESSY'S
Hessy's Music Store then was "the meet"
Tucked away on a Liverpool Street
They'd try out the goods
Couldn't buy, wished they could
But the owner was ever so neat

THE JACARANDA
In Liverpool, Jacaranda became
A place where the Fabs pursued fame
A club so unique
Where the music would speak
And cool was the name of the game

With art on the walls' beatnik scene
A creative hub where dreams convene
The Beatles would play
By night or by day
In Jacaranda's bohemian sheen

Though time's passed and days have
since flown
The Jac's cherished mem'ry has grown
In Liverpool's heart
It's a creative part
A legend where rock's seeds were sown

NEMS
In NEMS the fan story first started
The teens with their money soon parted
A young fan was looking
Trying to track down their booking
Imagine his joy when they charted?

MATHEW STREET
Mathew Street in the City's domain
Where music and history entertain
With Cavern Club's fame
Beatles' rise to acclaim
In that hot spot their legacy's plain

The sounds of guitars and young dreams
In the Cavern's dimly lit beams
A rock 'n' roll scene
Where history's been
Mathew Street echoes with musical
themes

So take a stroll down that lane

Where the Fab Four's star did sustain
And Mathew Street's lore
Forever will endure
In Liverpool's heart, it remains

PENNY LANE
A Barber's a Bus Stop, some shops
Make Penny Lane "Top of the Stops"
For fans on the run
Who just wanna have fun
And say that they vote it "The Tops"

On Penny Lane in Liverpool's heart
A place where memories still impart
A barber shop and bank
And a fireman to thank
Beatles' lyrics were just works of art

JFK (JOHN F. KENNEDY AIRPORT, NEW
YORK)
'64, at JFK they did land
The Beatles, an unknown rock band
With fans in a craze
They set New York ablaze
Their arrival, a moment so grand

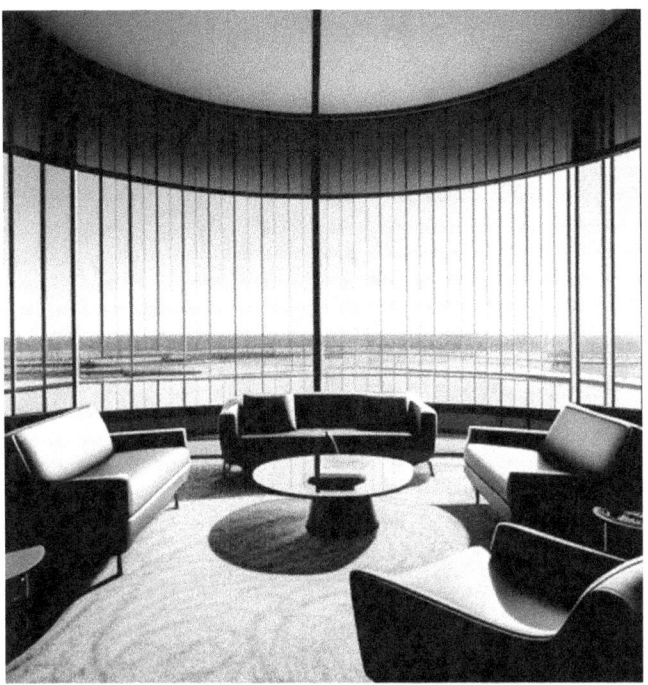

At the airport, a frenzy of screams
As they stepped off the plane so it seems
With hair that would sway
Began their first stay
In the land of American dreams

From Scouseland to JFK they'd arrive
In Beatlemania's whirlwind, they'd thrive
They took them by storm
And their welcome was warm
The Beatles, in history, they'd drive

ABBEY ROAD

The Beatles all loved Abbey Road
'Twas there that their talent first showed
WIth Sir George as their guide
They had no need to hide
And their records began to explode

Tourists flock both from near and afar
On that crossing they feel like a star
They pose and they stride
With a real Beatles pride
Just please don't get hit by a car!

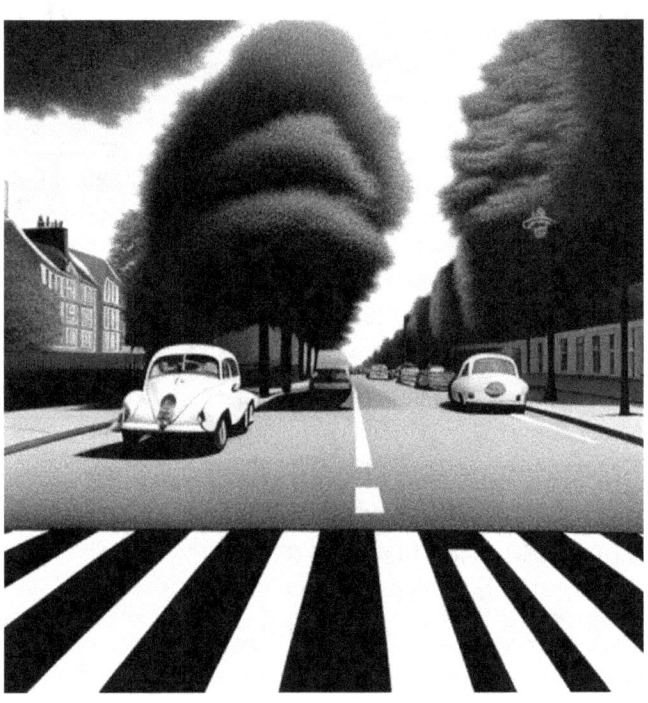

In that mansion where history was made
With melodies never to fade
Zebra crossing, a sight
Gathering fans day and night
Their legacy never betrayed

CARNABY STREET
This street in the sixties was prime
Where groovy fab fads ruled the time
With fashions so bold
A sight to behold
In London's scene truly sublime.

Psychedelia was really the rage
With everyone on the same page
With love what we need
And maybe some weed
No matter what gender or age

SHEA STADIUM
At Shea Stadium, cheers filled the air
The Beatles' fans pulling their hair
In '65, such a sight
Beatlemania's height
A historic gig beyond compare

In the heart of New York, they played
Beatles' music, the crowd's hearts swayed
With screaming and cheers
They conquered their fears

At Shea Stadium, memories made

Though the stadium's now part of the past
Those Shea gigs forever will last
In music's grand story
The fame and the glory
A chapter that's still unsurpassed

BLUE JAY WAY
Blue Jay Way had a mystical fate
George's guest had got lost and was late
So to while away time
He mixed music and rhyme
The result was this music, so great

3 SAVILE ROW
Apple Records, where music would flow
At Savile Row, London's grand show
With the Beatles in command
A creative wonderland,
Where melodies and dreams would
bestow

In the heart of the city so fine
Their HQ was a place of design
They processed such art
Simply right from the start
Apple Records, where stars would align

Now a part of rock history's grace

Where they first found their own special space
At Savile Row's door
The Beatles, forevermore
Left a legacy none can erase

HOLLYWOOD WALK OF FAME
Their stars on the great Walk of Fame
Make fans' finding Fabs quite a game
It's a famous location
To see on vacation
Take selfies, and clock every name.

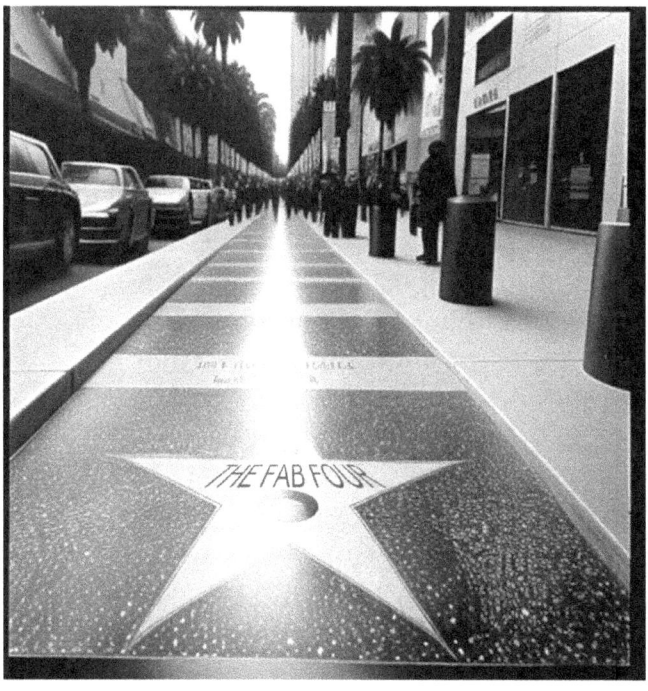

THE 2 STRAWBERRY FIELD(S)

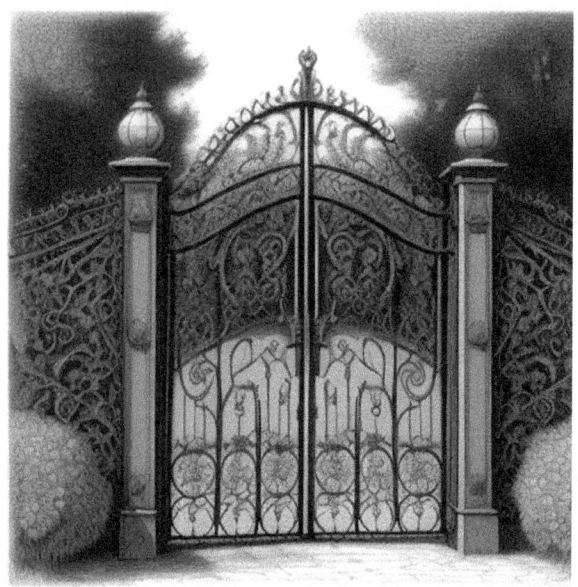

In Strawberry Fields, a domain
Where John's childhood dreams once did reign
John found inspiration
In the grounds of Salvation
With memories that forever remain

But across the Atlantic there grew
A counterpart tribute so true
In Central Park's heart
Strawberry Fields is the start
A place of peace where memories grew

In the 'Pool and New York, side by side
Two Strawberry Fields, world's divide
From John's vision they sprout
Different lands, there's no doubt
A future for hope and pure pride.

The 'Pool's Strawberry Field is Forever
The Salvation Army's endeavour
From John's early days
To its present-day phase
And its impact is really quite clever

THE DAKOTA

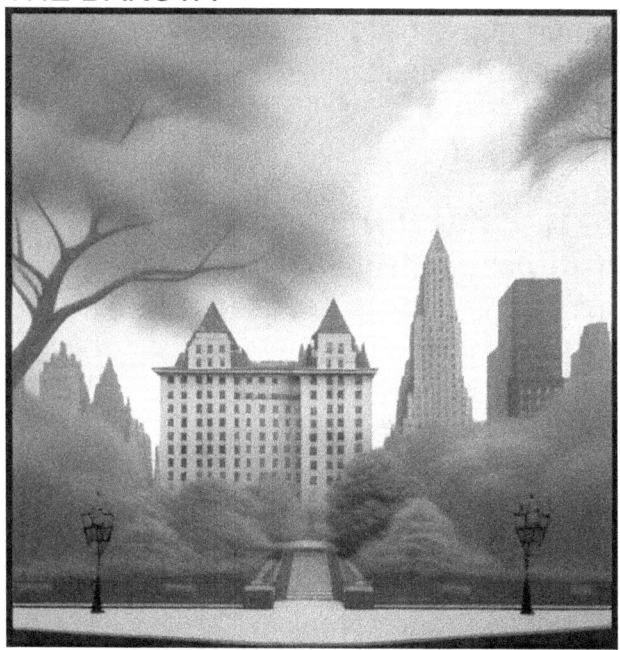

In Manhattan's Dakota, a sight
A building with stories and might
Its history so grand
In New York's urban land
It stands as a symbol of light

With Gothic-style charm, it's renowned
Where famous names once did abound
John Lennon did dwell
In its storied hotel
Where much art and life can be found

The Dakota, an icon to see
In Manhattan's historic decree
Its tales still persist
In the city's grand twist
A landmark that'll forever be

THE MULL OF KINTYRE
Where waves crash on rugged terrain
Where nature's pure beauty does reign
With vistas so high
Where the sea meets the sky
The Mull of Kintyre will remain.

In the Highlands of Scotland, it's found
A place where the heart is unbound
With landscapes so wild
Nature's essence compiled
It's here all your dreams are unwound.

THE LIVER BIRDS

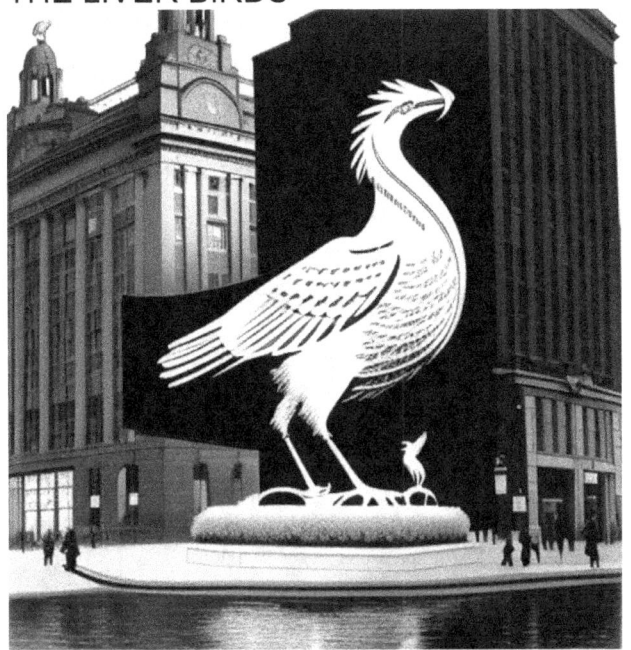

The Livers are two famous birds
Who are frequently covered by turds
Their chief claim to fame
How the town got its name
Still honoured and feted by herds

LIVERPOOL AIRPORT
Speke Airport was renamed John Lennon
So fans would fly in there from then on
To honour his name
Every season they came
And then bring the music to Zen on

LIVERPOOL MUSEUMS

The 'Pool has the greatest Museums
They're too good to miss you must see 'em
It'll boggle your mind
All the things you can find
And pay only just a per diem

THE ED SULLIVAN THEATER

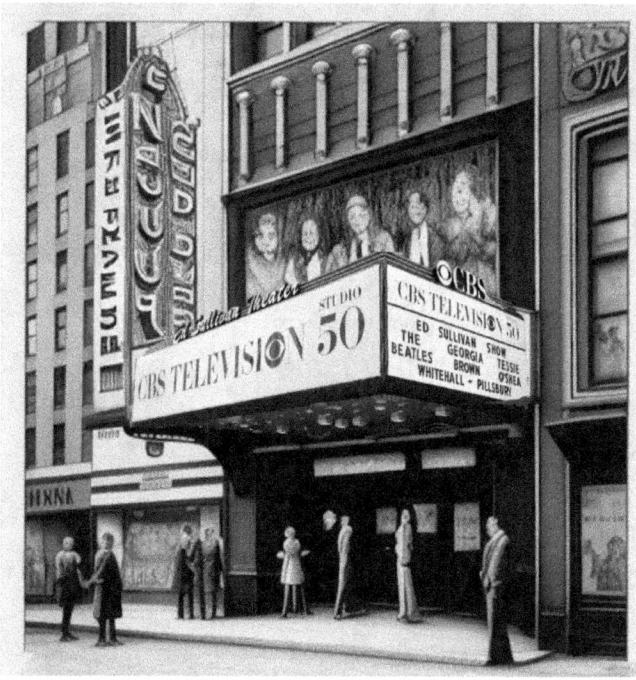

The Ed Sullivan Theater, renowned

In New York a true hallowed ground
Where legends have played
On its stage, dreams displayed
With history that truly astounds

In the heart of the city so bright
Ed Sullivan Theater's a sight
Where laughter and song
Have danced all night long
In the Big Apple's e're glowing limelight

CHAPTER 9 – MACCA'S BAND

ABE LABORIEL JR.
Abe Laboriel Paul's drummer is great
He'll always step up to the plate
He has so much power
He's a man of the hour
Performance is always first rate

BRIAN RAY
Brian Ray's on guitar and on bass
Does vocals too keeping apace
He loves what he does
Always feeling the buzz
Expressing delight on his face

RUSTY ANDERSON
Rusty sure is the man on guitar
His talent has taken him far
His performance takes flight
And we know he's just right
Adding magic to every bar

WIX WICKENS
Wix tackles the keyboards with might
Watch him go, he's a proper delight
Plus he works as M.D.
And it's so plain to see
That he guides the band through every nigh
.

CHAPTER 10 - 60'S & 70'S POP CULTURE ICONS

GERRY MARSDEN

And close on their heels there was Gerry
With his ditty 'bout Merseyside's Ferry
The fans all adored him
And this never bored him
To the end he remained always merry

ELTON JOHN

Elton John is a legend so bright
In music he's reached a great height
On keyboards he'd play
In a dazzling array
His songs a true source of delight

In costumes he'd always astound
Feathers sequins and shades that abound
With "Rocket Man" he'd soar
To the crowd's loud encore
In glitter and glam he was crowned

In "Goodbye Yellow Brick Road" Elton's ode
To fame's glitz and glamour he showed
He sang with such grace
In that timeless embrace
A classic that never grows old!

From "Candle" way back to "Your Song"
His musical prowess so strong
Sir Elton the star
With songs near and far
Makes people together feel strong

ROD STEWART

Rod Stewart the pop star so bold
With his raspy voice stories untold
Rocked the stage with such flair
With his wild spiky hair
In the music world he is pure gold!

In his youth he was quite the heartthrob
With his charm he could easily rob
Any heart that he chose
With his songs and his prose
In the realm of rock 'n' roll he'd hobnob

Now a legend his fame still endures
Singing ballads and rock he ensures
That his music lives on
Like a fine aged bourbon
Rod Stewart the icon still tours!

KEITH MOON

Keith Moon a wild man of drums
With antics that left us in thrums *(look it up!)*
He'd play with such flair

Toss his sticks in the air
His energy left us in chums (ditto line 2)

In The Who he would cause quite a fuss
With drumming that truly was plus
He'd crash and he'd bang
A rock 'n' roll gang
His style was a circus no fuss

But Moon's life was marked by a haze
His antics a wild fiery blaze
He partied so hard
It left him quite scarred
A legend in so many ways!

RYAN WHITE - DIRECTOR OF GOOD OL'
FREDA
Ryan White a producer with flair
In Hollywood he's a true player
With scripts that inspire
He sets hearts on fire
And his movies are beyond compare

From indie features he steers
Through triumphs and even through tears
He's got the right touch
And makes stories clutch
The hearts of all moviegoers' cheers

In Tinseltown quite the sensation
Bringing dreams to life no hesitation
With vision and grace
He'll conquer the race
Ryan White a true film sensation

SANDIE SHAW

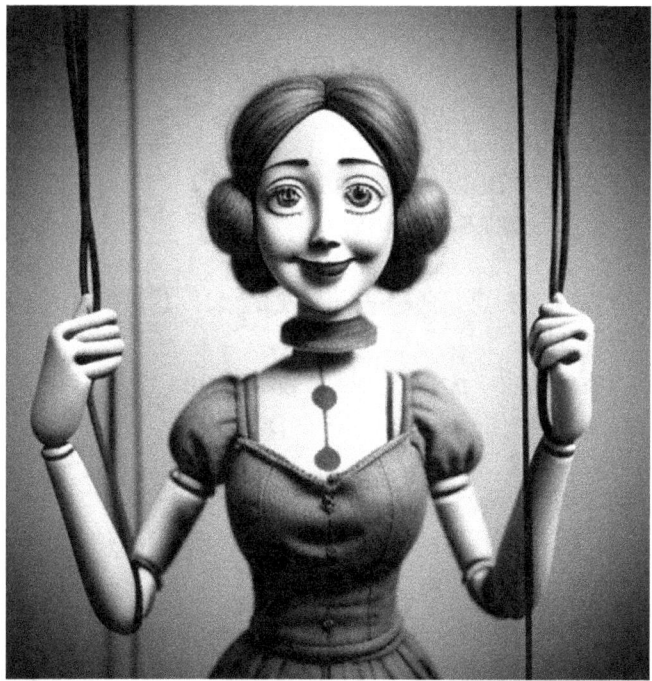

Sandie Shaw with her voice so divine
In British pop once a goldmine
With her songs she'd enthrall
In the sixties stood tall
In her barefoot chic she'd always shine

On the charts she would often be seen
In her style she was truly the queen
With her hair wild and free
She would sing with such glee
Pop sensation upon the world scene

 "Puppet" and then "Long Live Love"
Her melodies soared high above
Her smile was so bright
She would light up the night
Sandy Shaw is a star we all love

LULU
Her design was so stylish and chic
With a flair that was truly unique
In the midst of the crowd
She stood out bold and proud
Work of art that would never grow weak

Now Lulu's a legend you see
In the world of the pop stars she is key
With her warm Scottish sass
Such a lovable lass
And proving that love sets you free!

CILLA BLACK
She captured the hearts of her City
From singing her very first ditty
Her voice was commanding

Left others all standing
And charmed them all cos she was pretty

In Scouseland her talent did bloom
In showbiz she found her own room
With charm and with grace
She won hearts in each place
In her presence there was never a gloom

Her posters adorned every wall
In the '60s she captured them all
With her songs and TV
She brought joy you'll agree
Cilla Black loved by one and by all

DAVID CASSIDY
David a teen heartthrob's name
In the '70s he rose to great fame
With his charm and his style
He'd drive fans really wild
And rose to great heights of acclaim

With a voice that could melt every heart
On "The Partridge Family" he'd play a part
With those dreamy green eyes
He reached for the skies
On the music scene one work of art

His fame as the story is told
With successes the stress would unfold

He faced highs and lows
In the media's throes
An idol's tale stirring and bold

DAVID ESSEX
David Essex with charisma so bright
British pop star a beacon of light
With hits that would soar
And fans by the score
He dazzled the world with his might

In the '70s his music took flight
On stage he'd perform every night
With talent and flair
As his songs filled the air
David's star truly burned oh-so-bright

TWIGGY
Twiggy she was a model so sweet
With her manner so truly elite
In the Sixties she'd reign
Frame a global campaign
She was cute from her head to her feet

Her doe-eyed allure was the key
To the covers of Vogue you'll agree
With her pixie-like grace
In the fashion world's race
Her legacy so clear to see

From modelling she'd cross to the screen
In acting her talent was keen
With charm and with grace
She'd light up the place
Twiggy a star forever pristine

DUDLEY MOORE
Dudley Moore with his humour so sly
With his comedy reached for the sky
From "Beyond the Fringe"
When his future would hinge
And laughter and wit would fly high

In "Arthur" he played the rich drunk
With a charisma that left us all sunk
His piano keys danced
In films he entranced
And dear Dudley he never would flunk

Though he's gone from this world it is true
Dudley legacy's still shining through
HIs performance he'd bless
With such joy and finesse
In his laughter will forever accrue

DUSTY SPRINGFIELD
Dusty Springfield her voice pure as gold
In the music scene tales often told
She'd soulfully croon
She'd conquer the moon

Her voice was a joy to behold

She released "Son of a Preacher Man"
Made fans swoon as part of the plan
With style and with grace
In the pop world's embrace
Dusty Springfield an iconic Grand Dame

JOHN CLEESE

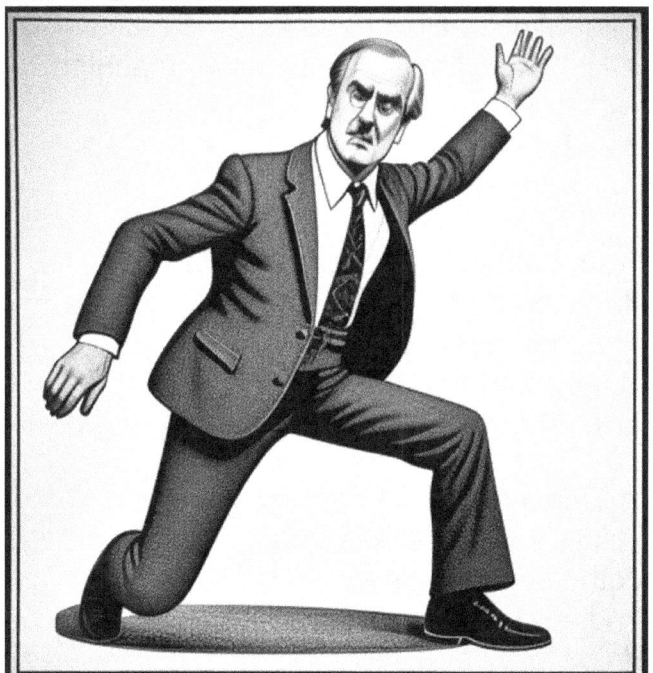

John Cleese with humour so tall
In Monty Python he'd give his all
With his Silly Walks
And mad Python talks

He'd make audiences laugh and enthrall

From Fawlty Towers he'd serve up delight
As "Basil the crazed" – what a sight!
With chaotic routines
And outrageous scenes
Cleese's genius is at comedy's height

ELLIOT MINTZ
Elliot Mintz a PR pro so keen
In Hollywood he's a well-known machine
With charm and finesse
He'd handle the press
In a world of big stars HE'S the scene

From Lennon to Yoko he'd guide
Handling both their careers side by side
A trusted confidant
In the media's haunt
Elliot Mintz's counsel they'd confide

In Tinseltown's glitz and its glare
Elliot's expertise was rare
With secrets to keep
And stories so deep
He's Hollywood's PR guru with flair

NEIL INNES
Neil Innes with talent so rare
A British composer with flair

From the Bonzo Dog Band
To Python's zany strand
His creativity filled the air

In "The Rutles" a spoof quite divine
He parodied music so fine
With Beatlesque style
He'd make the fans smile
A musical gem in his prime

Though he's gone now, his legacy stays
In his music and humour always
Neil Innes we cheer
For your laughter and cheer
In the world of comedy you blazed

PETULA CLARK
Petula Clark is a star of the stage
Even as a young child she'd engage
With a voice sweet and clear
She'd bring joy and cheer
In the world of music she'd wage

"Downtown" to "Don't Sleep in the Subway"
Her hits would brighten any dull day
With a vocal so fine
In every line
Petula's music would sweep us away

Though time marches on still she shines
In the spotlight her talent defines
Petula Clark evergreen
A timeless royal queen
She gets better just like a fine wine

SIR TIM RICE
Sir Tim Rice a lyrical king
With words he can make our hearts sing
With the "Lion King's" roar
His words we adore
In the musical world he's the thing!

He's penned tales of pharaohs and queens
In "Joseph" and "Jesus" routines
While Sir Andrew Lloyd's tunes
Wile away afternoons
They're truly creative machines

Mrs. McCartney's Liverpool Limericks
& Other Random Irish Haikus

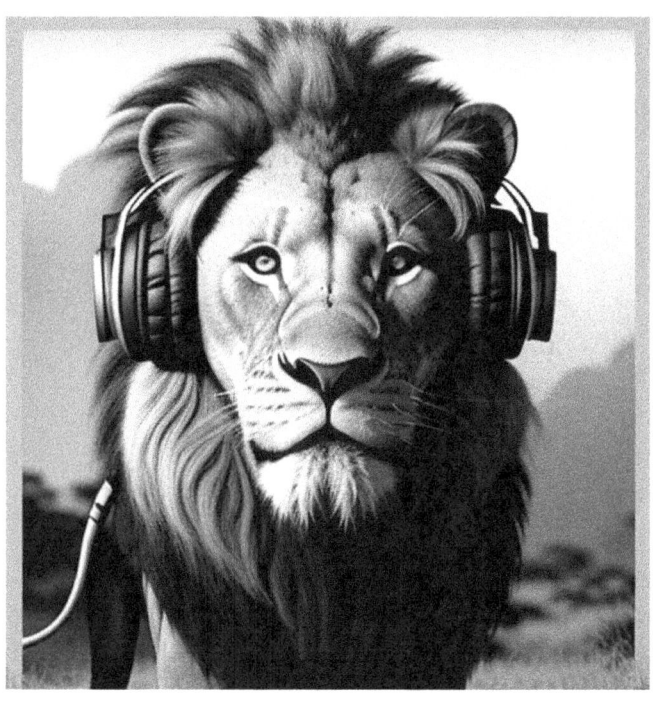

CHAPTER - 11 AND IN THE END

In the studio the boys took their stand
Crafting tunes with a flair for the grand
In A.I.'s techy embrace
"Now and Then" found its place
Beatles' single was not really planned

With computers their voices soared high
The Fab Four again making us cry
Through the circuits they croon
A harmonious tune
Their music forever will fly

Now and Then is a global delight
A.I. making their tune pure and bright
Their song a cascade
In the virtual parade
A masterpiece with every byte

So this limerick tells us the tale
Now and Then making one final sail
With their loving embrace
Once more finding their space
Came their swan song on another scale

I hope you had fun with my ditties
'Bout Liverpool and other great cities
Of music and fun
Even Band on the Run
But if you did not - what a pity!

And now my personal favourite limerick ever by Anon.

There was a young lady from Bude
Who went for a swim in the LAKE
A man in a punt stuck a pole in her EAR
And said "you can't swim here it's private"

Don't forget to tip your waitress

On these final pages you'll find codes to connect with my other ventures, Books, Tea, Dessert Wines/cocktail mixers and CBD. Hope you enjoy.

Love,

Angie McCartney

Dr. Angie

New Book for 2024, with 168 "Beatle People", their stories, Q&A and QR links to some videos, with digital illustration by Ruth McCartney and a fab cover by Shannon (www.ArtistShannnon.com). Published by Imagine & Wonder.

Order at
www.ThereAreFacesIRemember.com

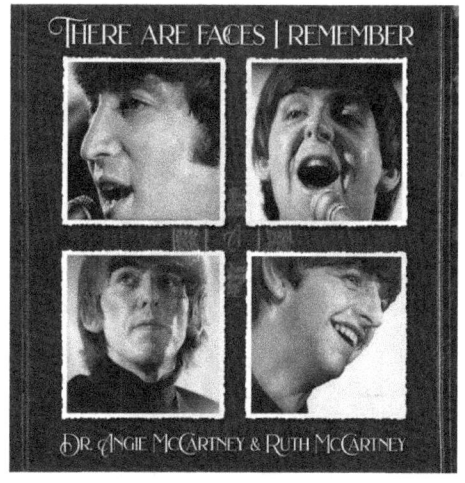

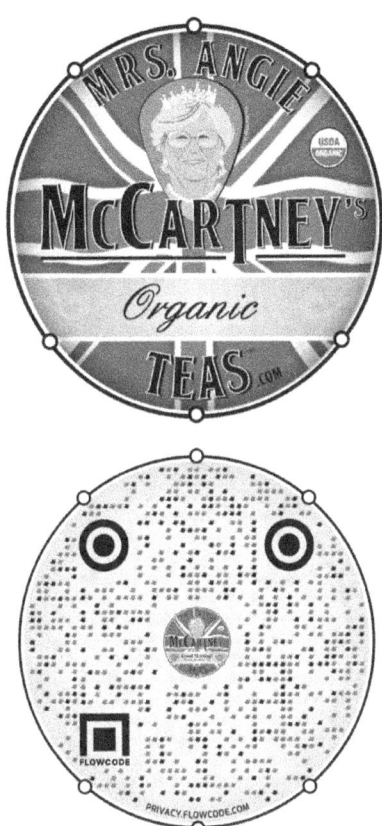

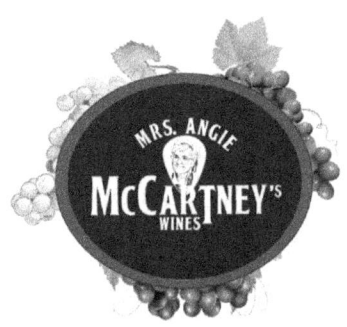

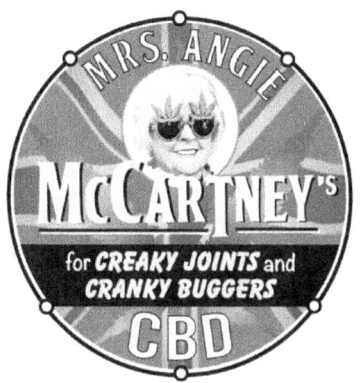

Tune in on Tuesdays at 11:30am Pacific on
Facebook.com/DrAngieMcCartney

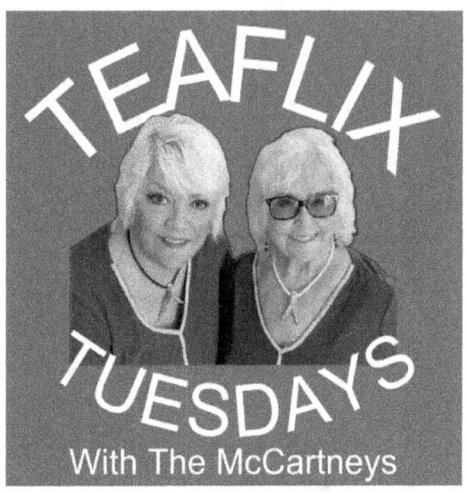

Or catch past episodes by scanning the
code.

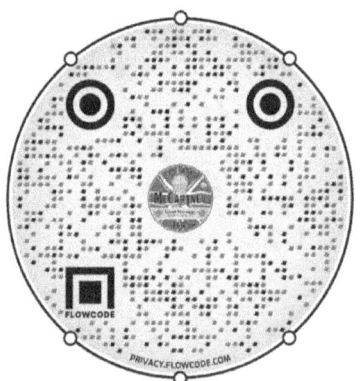

ABOUT THE AUTHOR

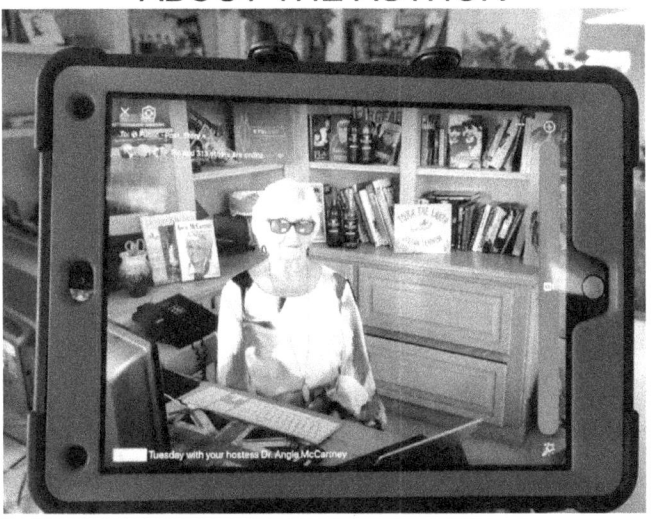

Born one month after the Wall Street crash in November of 1929, author & entrepreneur Dr. Angie McCartney has had tea with billionaires and busboys and done the laundry of rock stars and renegades. Now in her 90's she runs several online businesses and resides in Playa del Rey, California with her daughter Ruth and son-in-law Martin Nethercutt.

A Little Space for Your Notes